Mapping Our World

Maps and Mapmaking

by
Fran Sammis

Benchmark Books

MARSHALL CAVENDISH

NEW YORK

Marshall Cavendish Corporation
99 White Plains Road
Tarrytown, New York 10591-9001

© Marshall Cavendish Corporation 2000

Series created by Blackbirch Graphics, Inc.

Printed in Hong Kong

Photo Credits
Pages 12, 16–17, 19, 21, 25, 27 and 28: ©North Wind Picture Archives; page 30, 44, 47, and 48: ©U.S. Geological Survey; page 33: ©Library of Congress; pages 34: ©American Philosophical Society; pages 36 and 37: ©Perry-Castaneda Library Map Collection/University of Dallas at Austin; page 42: ©Archive Photos; page 46: ©U.S. Department of Commerce; page 50 and 53: ©NASA; page 51: ©Earth & Space Photos; page 54: ©Los Alamos National Library.

Library of Congress Cataloging-in-Publication Data
Sammis, Fran
        Maps and mapmaking / by Fran Sammis
            p.   cm. — (Mapping our world)
        Includes bibliographical references and index.
        Summary: Discusses the history and importance of maps and the science of cartography.
        ISBN 0-7614-0367-1
        1. Maps—Juvenile literature. 2. Cartography—Juvenile literature. [1. Maps.
2. Cartography.] I. Title. II. Series: Sammis, Fran. Mapping our world.
    GA130.S26   2000
    912—dc21
                                                                                    98-49883
                                                                                    CIP
                                                                                    AC

: Contents

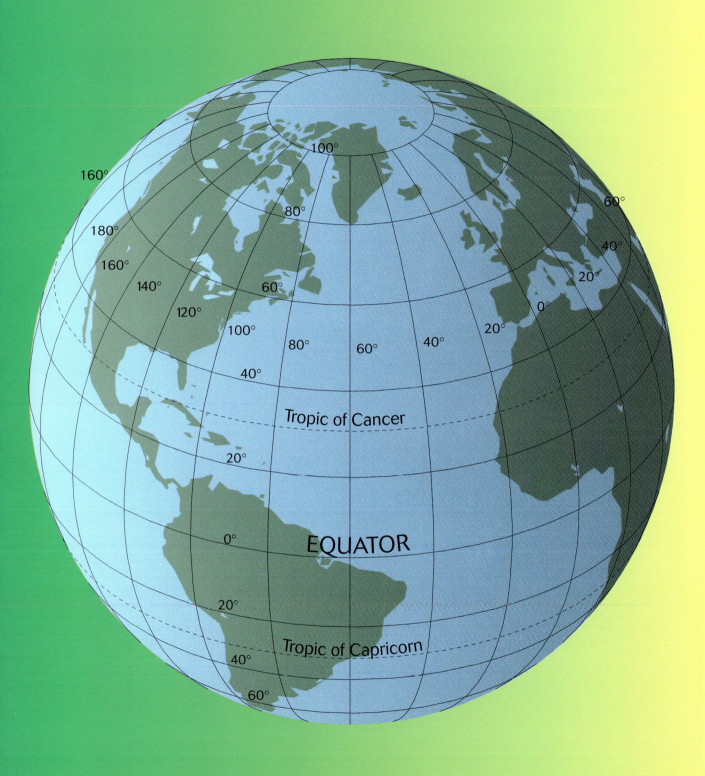

The Importance of Maps

As tools for understanding and navigating the world around us, maps are an essential resource. Maps provide us with a representation of a place, drawn or printed on a flat surface. The place that is shown may be as vast as the solar system or as small as a neighborhood park. What we learn about the place depends on the kind of map we are using.

Kinds of Maps

Physical maps show what the land itself looks like. These maps can be used to locate and identify natural geographic features such as mountains, bodies of water, deserts, and forests.

Distribution maps show where something can be found. There are two kinds of distribution maps. One shows the range or area a feature covers, such as a map showing where grizzly bears live or where hardwood forests grow.

The second kind of distribution map shows the density of a feature. That is, how much or how little of the feature is present. These maps allow us to see patterns in the way a feature is distributed. Rainfall and population maps are two examples of this kind of distribution map.

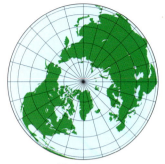
Globular

Mercator

Mollweide

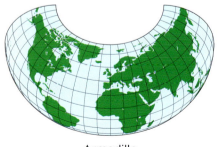
Armadillo

Political maps show us how an area is divided into countries, states, provinces, or other units. They also show where cities and towns are located. Major highways and transportation routes are also included on some kinds of political maps.

Movement maps help us find our way around. They can be road maps, street maps, and public transportation maps. Special movement maps called "charts" are used by airplane or boat pilots to navigate through air or on water.

Why Maps Are Important

Many people depend on maps to do their jobs. A geologist, for example, uses maps of Earth's structure to locate natural resources such as coal or petroleum. A transportation planner will use population maps to determine where new roads may need to be built.

A map can tell us how big a place is, where one place is in relation to another, what a place was like in the past, and what it's like now. Maps help us understand and move through our own part of the world and the rest of the world, too. Some maps even help us move through our solar system and universe!

Terms to Know

Maps are created and designed by incorporating many different elements and accepted cartographic (mapmaking) techniques. Often, maps showing the exact same area will differ from one another, depending upon the choice or critical elements, such as scale and projection. Following is a brief listing of some key mapmaking terms.

Projection. A projection is a way to represent the round Earth on a flat surface. There are a number of different ways to project, or transfer, round-Earth information to a flat surface, though each method results in some distortion. That is, areas may appear larger or smaller than they really are—or closer or farther apart. The maps on page 6 show a few varieties of projections.

Latitude. Lines of latitude, or parallels, run parallel to the equator (the imaginary center of Earth's circumference) and are used to locate points north and south of the equator. The equator is 0 degrees latitude, the north pole is 90 degrees north latitude, and the south pole is 90 degrees south latitude.

Longitude. Lines of longitude, or meridians, run at right angles to the equator and meet at the north and south poles. Lines of longitude are used to locate points east and west of the prime meridian.

Prime meridian. An imaginary line that runs through Greenwich, England; considered 0 degrees longitude. Lines to the west of the prime meridian go halfway around the world to 180 degrees west longitude; lines to the east go to 180 degrees east longitude.

Hemisphere. A half circle. Dividing the world in half from pole to pole along the prime meridian gives you the eastern and western hemispheres. Dividing the world in half at the equator gives you the northern and southern hemispheres.

Scale. The relationship of distance on a map to the actual distance on the ground. Scale can be expressed in three ways:

    1. As a ratio—1:63,360 (one inch equals 63,360 inches)

    2. Verbally—one inch equals one mile

    3. Graphically— [1 mi.]

Because 63,360 inches equal one mile, these scales give the same information: one map-inch equals one mile on the ground.

Large-scale maps show a small area, such as a city park, in great detail. Small-scale maps show a large area, such as an entire continent, in much less detail, and on a much smaller scale.

The Art and Process of Mapmaking

Maps have been made for thousands of years. Early maps, based on first-hand exploration, were some of the most accurate tools of their

◄◄ *Opposite: The maps shown here are just four of the many different projections in which the world can be displayed.*

225 million years ago

1

180 million years ago

2

65 million years ago

3

present day

4

time. Others, based on guesses about what an area was like, were often very beautiful, but were not especially accurate.

As technology—such as photography and flight—evolved, cartographers (mapmakers) were able not only to map most of Earth in detail, they were also able to make maps of our solar system.

To make a map today, cartographers first determine what a map is to show and who is most likely to use it. Then, they assemble the information they will need for the map, which can come from many different kinds of experts—such as meteorologists, geologists, and surveyors—as well as from aerial photography or satellite feedback.

Mapping a Changing Earth

If you traced around all the land masses shown on a world map, then cut them out and put them together like a jigsaw puzzle, the result would look something like map 1 at the top of this page. Scientists think this is how Earth looked about 225 million years ago.

Over time, this single continent, Pangaea (Pan–JEE–uh), slowly broke apart into two land masses called Laurasia and Gondwanaland (map 2). Maps 3 and 4 show how the land masses continued to break up and drift apart over millions of years, until the continents assumed the shapes and positions we recognize today. Earth has not, however, finished changing.

Scientists have established that Earth's surface is made up of sections called tectonic plates. These rigid plates, shown in the map on page 9, are in

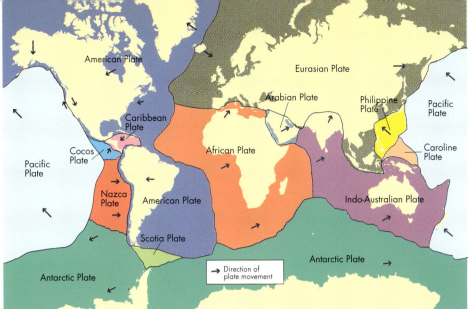

slow, constant motion, moving from 1/4 to 1 inch a year. As they move, they take the continents and sea floors with them. Sometimes, their movements cause disasters, such as earthquakes and volcanic activity.

After many more millions of years have passed, our Earth's continents will again look very different from what we know today.

Reading a Map

In order for a map to be useful, it must be the right kind of map for the job. A small-scale map of Illinois would not help you find your way around Chicago; for that, you would need a large-scale map of the city. A physical map of North America would not tell you where most of the people live; you would need a distribution map that shows population.

Once you have found the right map, you will need to refer to the map legend, or key, to be sure you are interpreting the map's information correctly. Depending on the type of map, the legend tells the scale used for the map, and notes the meaning of any symbols and colors used.

In their most basic form, maps function as place finders. They show us where places are, and we use these maps to keep from getting lost. But as you have begun to see, maps can tell us much more about our world than simply where places are located. Just how much more, you'll discover in the chapters ahead.

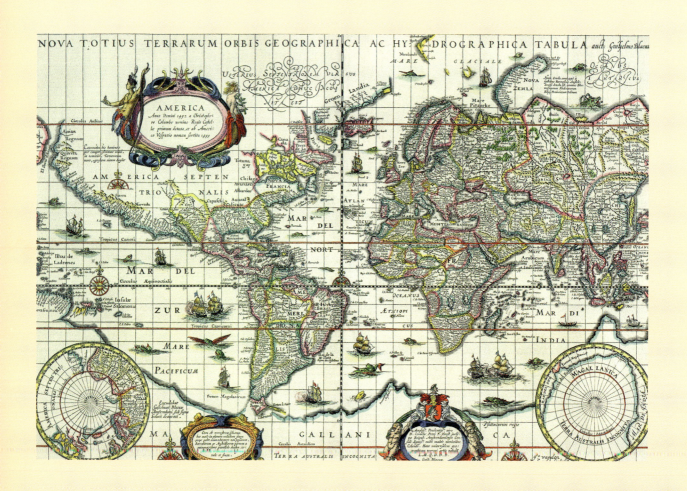

Early Mapmaking

Maps are so much a part of our lives today we don't give them a second thought. Weather maps on TV and in the newspapers help us plan our activities. Road maps help us get quickly from place to place. The "You Are Here" map at the mall tells you how close you are to the video store. Even computer games contain maps of imaginary worlds to be conquered.

Because of maps, we know what our world—and others—look like. We know that Italy is shaped like a boot and the Great Lakes make Michigan's lower peninsula look like a mitten. We know that there are mountains in Asia and deserts in Australia. We can study the bottom of the ocean without getting anywhere near the water and check out the craters on the moon without putting on a space suit. We can count the volcanoes on Mars and locate stars in the sky. All thanks to maps.

Maps have existed for thousands of years, but the earliest maps weren't commonly available. Nor were they detailed, wide-ranging, or accurate.

◀◀ *Opposite: This 1630 map of the world was based on a Mercator projection, introduced in 1569.*

The First Maps

Experts think that some cave drawings made by the earliest humans may have been maps. If this were true, it would mean that maps existed 37,000 years ago. There is no proof of this, however.

What we do know is that the Babylonians, living in what is now Iraq, made the oldest known map in 2300 B.C. This map was scratched on a clay tablet and shows someone's property, set in a river valley between two mountain ranges. An early Babylonian map of

▼ *Below:* Humans have been making maps for thousands of years. This ancient Babylonian map—made more than 3,000 years ago—shows one mapmaker's view of the world.

the world is shown at left. Egyptians were also among the first map-makers. The oldest existing Egyptian map dates to about 1300 B.C. and shows the site of a gold mine in what is now Sudan.

These maps showing property, towns, or other local areas were among the most common kinds of early maps. Maps of the world—the little of it that was known—would not have been as useful as local maps. Property maps, for example, were used by rulers to set tax rates for their subjects. It took the rise of ancient Greek civilization to spur an interest in knowing what the whole world looked like. Later, as explorers ventured forth to claim land, wealth, or fame for themselves and their countries, world maps became more important.

The Greeks and Romans

By the 500s B.C., Greece was the center for scientific study and learning in the ancient world. The Greeks' geographic studies and mapmaking influenced cartographers for more than 1,500 years. As others had done before them, early Greek cartographers described and mapped their own territories. But they also mapped as much of the rest of the world as they could piece together through travel and their knowledge of astronomy and mathematics. Maps were a common feature of ancient Greek life. Although none of those early maps have survived, we know about them from the many ancient Greek writings that describe them.

Most people at that time thought that Earth was flat. The Greeks, however, described a round Earth and debated the size of it. About 200 B.C., Eratosthenes, a poet and mathematician, calculated that Earth measured 25,000 miles (40,233 kilometers) around its circumference. He was amazingly close to the true circumference, which is 24,902 miles (40,075 kilometers). Later Greek scientists criticized Eratosthenes's calculations, however, and ended up using a figure of 18,000 miles (28,967 kilometers) for Earth's circumference. This mistake was to have a long-lasting effect on both mapmaking and on the navigators who used maps.

The Roman Empire

By 75 B.C. the Roman Empire was in power. At its height, this empire covered an enormous amount of territory. It stretched all around the Mediterranean Sea, taking in the area from present-day Great Britain to what is now Turkey, as well as the north coast of Africa, including Egypt.

The Romans built roads throughout Europe and made many maps detailing these lines of communication, travel, and conquest. They also constructed military maps and, like ancient Egyptians and Greeks, mapped personal property for tax purposes.

However, unlike the Greeks, the Romans did not have an interest in trying to map areas outside their territory. The size and shape of the whole world was not as important to them as their own piece of it. But one of the subjects of the Roman Empire, a Greek living in Alexandria, Egypt, had a very keen interest in the world and wanted to share it with others.

Ptolemy

Ptolemy was the most important cartographer during the time of the Roman Empire. About A.D. 150, Ptolemy wrote an eight-volume work called *Geography*. Here he collected and set forth the information that was already known about the world and added discoveries and inventions of his own.

While earlier Greeks had determined that Earth was round, not flat, it was Ptolemy who worked out projections. He was the first to do so, though not the last. Examples of different styles of projection can be seen in the maps on pages 10, 22–23, and 48–49.

Ensuring Greater Accuracy

Ptolemy also worked with the concept of scale, relating distance on a map to the actual distance on the ground. It had been a common practice for cartographers to size areas differently—even those shown on a single map. They based the size of an area on how much was known about it. The more that was known, the more items, such as place names, there were to include. This meant that Europe might end up larger than Africa, about which Europeans of Ptolemy's time knew very little.

Ptolemy felt that maps should reflect the sizes of different regions in relation to one another. The problem was how to do this and still provide all the information included on existing maps. Ptolemy's solution was to show an overview—"a world map"—and then a series of regional maps that could be larger or smaller, depending on how much needed to be included. This is still the way we structure atlases today—almost 2,000 years later!

Although earlier Greek cartographers had occasionally used some lines of latitude and longitude, they were used mostly to orient the maps rather than to locate places on them. Ptolemy correctly insisted that using latitude and longitude to locate places was the only way to ensure that maps were accurate. If a place was "pinned down" by its latitude and longitude, it could be properly placed (and found) on all maps.

Ptolemy was the first cartographer to set up a systematic grid of latitude and longitude lines resembling those we're used to seeing on maps today. His coordinates were not particularly accurate, but the concept of a regular grid was an important one in the history of cartography.

Ptolemy's Mistakes

As valuable as the information in Ptolemy's *Geography* was, he made several mistakes that would affect mapmaking and exploration more than a thousand years later. At the time Ptolemy made his maps, the known world consisted of most of Europe, southern and southwestern Asia, and northern Africa. Mapmakers had to guess at the size and shape of places Europeans had not as yet explored. As a result, Ptolemy made Asia much larger than it is. You can see this distortion on the copy of a map made by Ptolemy on pages 16–17.

▶ *Right:* This is a copy, made in 1472, of a map that Ptolemy first created in A.D. 150. The most recognizable places are Western Europe and the Mediterranean region, on the western side of the map. Note the twelve wind heads around the border.

Since the known continents were mainly situated in the northern hemisphere, Ptolemy invented a huge landmass called *Terra Australis Incognita*, or "Unknown Southern Land," to balance them. Ptolemy guessed that this land—like a very much bigger Antarctica—covered the bottom of Earth. He thought *Terra Australis* had to exist, or the world would be top-heavy and tip over.

In addition to overestimating land areas, Ptolemy underestimated the total size of Earth. He assumed Earth's circumference was 18,000 miles (28,967 kilometers), which is just under three-fourths as big as it really is. When he drew his world maps, the western edge of Europe ended up only a small ocean away from the eastern edge of Asia. No one knew that two more continents (North and South America) and an immense ocean (the Pacific) lay westward between Europe and Asia. In fact, Ptolemy's idea of the world's size left no room for all of this unknown territory to exist.

Thirteen hundred years later, Columbus counted on the accuracy of Ptolemy's world view as he set out for what he thought would be a short journey west to Asia.

The Middle Ages

During the Middle Ages, about A.D. 400–1450, scientific learning became less important than religion. And maps of that time reflected this change. The center of the Christian faith was Jerusalem, so that city often occupied the center of a world map. Because paradise was thought to lie eastward, east was located at the top of a map, in the direction of Heaven. In addition, Biblical places such as the Garden of Eden shared map space with actual cities.

Maps were often wonderfully colored and decorated with fanciful people and animals. Although world maps were more pretty than practical, two very useful kinds of local maps were produced during the Middle Ages. There were road maps showing people the way to holy shrines and cities. An example is the twelfth-century map showing the way to Jerusalem (see opposite). And there were portolan

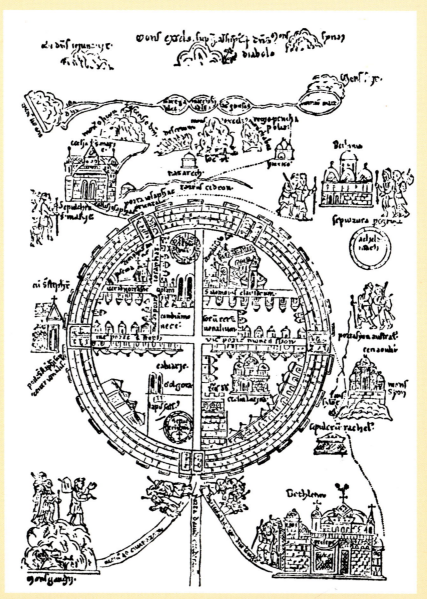

▲ **Above:** *This twelfth-century map made in Brussels shows the various routes pilgrims could follow to Jerusalem.*

charts—maps for navigators. The oldest existing portolan dates from the late 1200s. However, people had been sailing the seas and mapping them long before that.

The Navigators

From the earliest days, ocean travelers depended heavily on their knowledge of winds and currents to make their trips easier and faster. Polynesian vessels sailed the South Pacific as early as 1000 B.C., navigating huge expanses of open water to move from island to island. They kept track of the geography and weather conditions during their voyages by making stick maps. Reeds were tied together to make a frame. More reeds were crisscrossed inside the frame, some curved and others at an angle. The direction of these sticks signified currents and wind directions. Shells were added to show the locations of islands.

In a similar fashion, but 2,000 years later, portolan charts featured wind directions indicated by a series of crisscrossing lines. These early sea charts also included wind roses—circular designs divided into sections that showed the directions from which the winds blew. Drawing wind roses could be very simple—an arrangement of lines and arrows—or very elaborate. The fancier ones, and especially the ones divided into more than just four or eight sections, made people think of a rose.

During the Middle Ages, maps such as Ptolemy's were preserved by adventurous Arabs. As the period drew to a close, these maps were rediscovered by Europeans, and they prompted much exploration. As the great age of European exploration began to flourish in the late 1400s and early 1500s, navigators ventured farther and farther from the relative safety of the known world. In addition to great geographic discoveries, this led to new and more accurate maps of Earth. Two navigators of the time whose voyages drastically changed people's view of the world were Christopher Columbus and Ferdinand Magellan.

Christopher Columbus

Columbus made the historic 1492 voyage for Spain to chart a western trade route to Asia. He had carefully studied the world maps that were available and was convinced that his goal was easily attainable. After all, Europe and Asia were so close—only a small ocean separated them. Unfortunately, Columbus was counting on maps, such as Ptolemy's, which were based on an inaccurate measurement of Earth's circumference.

Columbus's voyage did not result in a new route to Asia, of course. Instead, Columbus began Europe's discovery of the Americas, which changed the map face of the world for all time. The "new" lands began showing up on maps by 1500. It was not until 1507, however, that a German mapmaker called this territory "America" in honor of the Italian navigator Amerigo Vespucci, who had made several voyages to South America.

Christopher Columbus

Ferdinand Magellan

Once the Americas were established on the maps of the day, Europeans continued looking westward for a route to Asia. In 1519, Spain sent Magellan to find a way through the newly discovered land mass and on to Asia. Magellan sailed to Brazil, then worked his way south along the eastern coast of South America until he passed through the strait—a narrow body of water—at the southern end of the continent. Having finally reached the Pacific Ocean, Magellan and his crew thought their voyage was almost over. No European had any idea of the real size of the Pacific.

Ferdinand Magellan

Instead of a short sail to Asia, it took 90 days before Magellan and his crew, suffering from extreme hunger and thirst, landed their ships on the Philippine Islands.

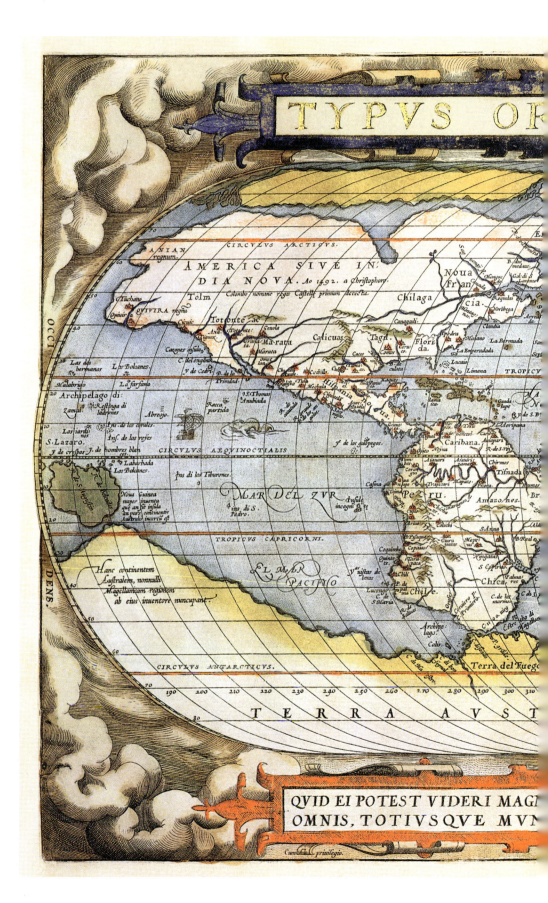

▶ *Right:* This world map was made in 1588 by Abraham Ortelius. Note Terra Australis Nondum Cognita—"Unknown Southern Land"—at the bottom of the map.

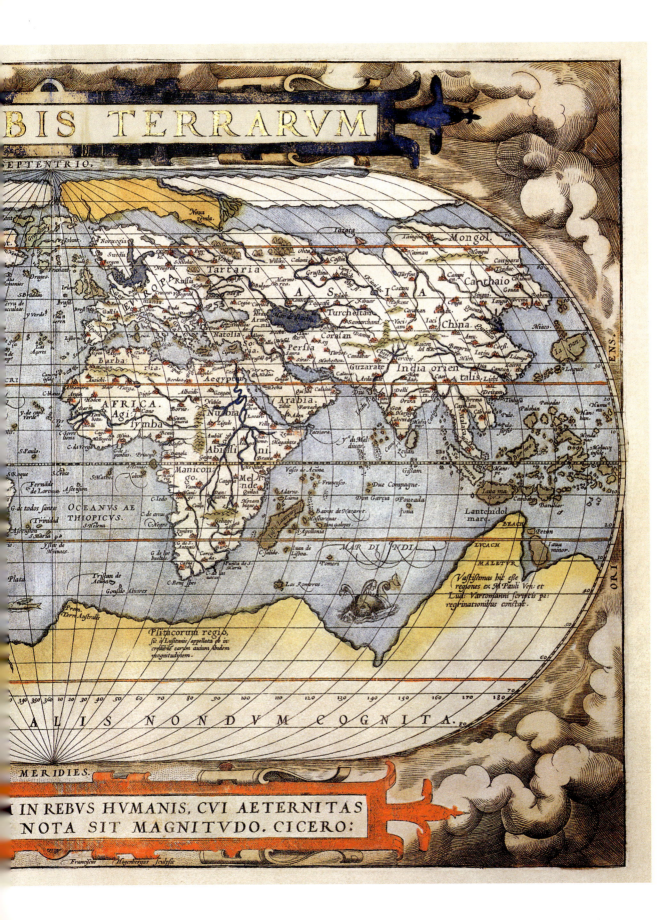

Magellan was killed there by the native islanders. One of his ships continued sailing west, however, and finally returned to Spain in 1522. Magellan's men were the first to circumnavigate the planet (sail around it completely). Finally, Earth's size could be understood.

A new version of the world was mapped by one of the members of Magellan's voyage, and soon the information appeared on other maps as well. To get some idea of how the world looked to people at that time, turn to the world map on page 22–23. This map was created in 1588 by the Dutch cartographer Abraham Ortelius. At a quick glance, the map looks quite similar to a world map of today. However, a closer look shows that some parts are very different: South America, for example, is not accurately drawn. And at the bottom of the map is a sprawling Unknown Southern Land, which Ptolemy had conceived nearly 1,400 years earlier!

The First Modern Atlas

The map you have just looked at is a copy of a map that appeared along with 70 others in a volume published by Ortelius in 1570. It was called the *Theatrum Orbis Terrarum* ("Theater of the World"). It is considered the first modern atlas. An atlas is a collection of maps bound into a single book. Before there were atlases, maps were collected loose in folders. Atlases were first put together by the Italians in the mid-1500s. Each volume was created as a special order for a single customer, who chose the maps to be included. Unlike the Italian atlases, the maps in Ortelius's volume had a standard appearance because Ortelius redrew them all from the originals. The book was printed in multiple copies so that more than one person could own one.

The first books of maps, including Ortelius's, did not have the word *atlas* in their titles. However, many volumes included a picture of Atlas—the giant from Greek mythology who held the world on his shoulders. The first book actually called an "atlas" was published in 1585 by the Belgian cartographer Gerardus Mercator.

The Mercator Projection

Mercator's most outstanding achievement was not his atlas, however, but a world map that he created in 1569. The map was laid out as a rectangle, so that the lines of latitude and longitude crossed each other at right angles. This was quite different from other maps of Mercator's time. They were either laid out as ovals, like Ortelius's map, or as circles. On an oval map, the lines of longitude curve rather than going straight up and down, and on a circular map (see pages 38–39) the lines of longitude *and* latitude curve.

Although Mercator's projection greatly distorted the size of the land masses, his map was extremely valuable to sailors, since it allowed them to easily plot straight-line courses across the oceans. By the 1600s, maps based on Mercator's projection were widely used by mariners. On page 10 is an example of a world map from this period, based on a Mercator projection. The Mercator projection is the most commonly used map projection today.

Tools for Mapmakers and Navigators

As navigators traveled the oceans and discovered new lands, they had to have some way of telling where they were so that their discoveries could be properly plotted on a map. Several tools came to be especially important in determining direction and position.

Compasses

Compasses were used in China in about A.D. 1000 and in Europe by the 1100s. The first mariner's compass was simply a magnetic needle mounted on a bit of wood or cork that floated in a bowl of water. By the 1200s, these early compasses were in general use by navigators. Some time later, probably in the 1300s, the needle was mounted on a wind rose,

An early compass

and the whole became a compass rose—a circle of points showing direction based on magnetic north. For this reason, north became the most important point and, to this day, the main direction noted by a map's compass rose.

Of course, a compass rose that is printed on a map differs from an actual compass in one important way. Both show the user which way is north—but not the same north. A printed compass rose points in the direction of true, or geographic, north: toward the North Pole. An actual compass points in the direction of magnetic north: a magnetic field that lies about 1,000 miles (1,600 kilometers) from the North Pole. One style of mariner's compass from the 1500s is shown in the illustration on page 25.

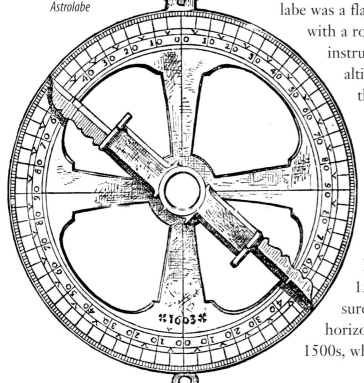

Astrolabe

Astrolabes

The Greeks invented the astrolabe in the second century B.C., and the Arabs refined it around A.D. 600. An astrolabe was a flat metal ring marked off in degrees, with a rotating bar in the center. This instrument could be used to measure the altitudes of stars, planets, the sun, and the moon. From such measurements it was possible to establish latitude. By holding the ring up, making sightings, and moving the center bar, navigators could measure the angle of the sun above the horizon. Comparing this measurement to charts, they could determine latitude. Navigators used astrolabes until the 1500s. They used astrolabes to measure the position of the sun above the horizon. Astrolabes were in use until the 1500s, when the cross-staff came into use.

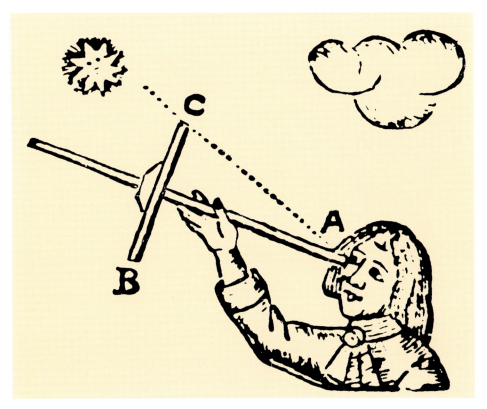

◀ *Left:* In order to use a
cross-staff, a navigator had
to look directly at the sun.

Cross-staffs

Like an astrolabe, a cross-staff could be used to measure the sun's
altitude and establish latitude. The cross-staff came to be preferred
by navigators, however, because it was easier to use on board a rolling
ship. The illustration above shows a navigator using a cross-staff.
The "staff" is the long rod and the "cross" is the short one. There
are eyeholes at points A, B, and C. A navigator looked through eyehole A, then moved the cross back and forth until eyehole B lined up
with the horizon and, at the same time, eyehole C lined up with the
sun. The position of the cross on the staff marked an angle that told
the altitude of the sun. From this, the navigator could determine his
latitude.

Although a cross-staff was easier to use than an astrolabe, the
drawback, as you can see from the illustration, was that you had to

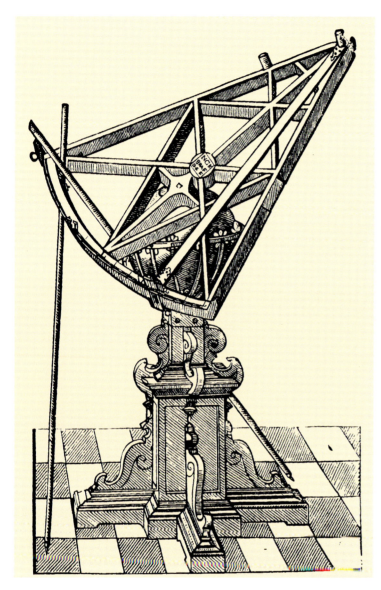

look directly into the sun when taking measurements. In 1595, the English explorer John Davis invented a new version known as the "backstaff," which was later refined as the "quadrant." Both the backstaff and quadrant could be used with one's back to the sun. This was a very important improvement in design. This version of the quadrant was still used by navigators as late as the 1700s.

Sextants

The sextant, pictured on the left, came into use in 1757. It gained favor with navigators because it was a bit smaller than the quadrant and easier to use. The sextant derived its name from the fact that it could measure up to a 60-degree angle, or one-sixth of a circle.

Chronometers

In 1714, the British parliament offered a reward to the first person who could invent a reliable way of measuring longitude at sea. It took until 1765 for an English watchmaker named John Harrison to come up with the right timepiece— the chronometer, perhaps the most important navigational tool that was developed. It was a clock that accurately measured time at sea. It was necessary to reliably establish the time in order to establish longitude.

▲ **Above:** *Like a cross-staff, a sextant measured the angle of the sun, which helped a navigator to figure out his latitude.*

The world is divided into 360 degrees of longitude which, in time, equals 24 hours. Therefore, 15 degrees of longitude are equal to one hour. A chronometer was set to whatever the baseline time was. That is the time at the prime meridian, which was 0 degrees longitude and was the point from which the longitude was measured. A navigator compared his locational time to "prime time," indicated by the chronometer. By knowing how much time had elapsed, he could determine how far east or west of 0 degrees longitude he had traveled and, thus, the longitude of his present position.

In 1884, Greenwich, England, was adopted as the international prime meridian. Before then, different countries used different places as their prime meridian. Usually it was the capital city. Therefore, the same area shown on different maps could have different longitude coordinates, depending on the mapmaker's nationality.

The importance of the chronometer was quickly noted. Captain James Cook used it on his Pacific explorations after 1772, allowing for the precise mapping of the Pacific islands for the first time.

For the next one hundred years, exploration increased as people set out to discover as much as possible about both new and old lands, as well as the oceans and seas connecting them. This, in turn, led to increased mapmaking efforts—both to guide explorers and to record their discoveries.

A Closer Look

Ptolemy invented *Terra Australis Incognita* ("Unknown Southern Land") in A.D. 150 to "balance" the world. Look again at the world map by Ortelius on pages 22–23. How does *Terra Australis* compare with Australia? What are the differences in size? In shape? What other major differences can you find between Ortelius's map and a modern one?

Chapter 2

The Birth of Modern Mapmaking

Exploration and mapmaking continued to advance in the 1700s and 1800s. During this period, the general public became more interested in the world beyond their own region—and in the maps that showed them the locations of newly discovered lands.

Surveying the Scene

The refinement of surveying techniques in France in the late 1600s and 1700s greatly improved the art of mapmaking. By measuring angles and distances between various points, surveyors can plot a picture of the part of Earth they are studying. They can learn its shape, size, and position. This information can then be used to set boundaries, or it can be translated into topographic maps.

Surveying has been used since ancient times. The Egyptians, for example, fixed the boundaries of their fields along the Nile River by surveying the land. The boundary markers could then be reestablished after the waters of the Nile receded at the end of the river's annual flood.

Beginning in 1676 and continuing until 1791, a family of astronomers and surveyors by the name of Cassini undertook the ambitious project of surveying all of France. When they started,

◀◀ *Opposite:* This is the northeast corner of a map of the United States and Canada made by a Connecticut silversmith in 1784.

determining longitude was still an inaccurate science. However, Jean-Dominique Cassini worked out a new way of calculating longitude that was much more precise than any method used up until then. It involved calculations based on the movements and eclipses of Jupiter's four largest moons. Cassini used the moons to calculate the correct time in Paris, which the French often used as the prime meridian. Then he figured out the difference between the time in Paris and the local time where he was surveying land. Knowing the difference between the two times helped Cassini calculate the longitude of the site he was surveying.

Surveyors who were trained in Cassini's method fanned out throughout France to take measurements and report back. In addition, people around the world used Cassini's technique to pinpoint locations, and then sent him the information. The Cassini family put all of the measurements on a huge world map. Gradually the map took on a shape that reflected, for the first time, the true proportions of land and seas. Scientific accuracy, rather than guesswork, became the new standard in mapmaking.

Mapmaking in the 1700s

As the 1700s progressed and the boundaries of the world came into better focus, explorers, scientists, and surveyors began the task of filling in those boundaries. Some explorers contributed only simple sketch maps showing roughly where they had been and what they had seen. Others, trained in survey techniques, provided details that remain on maps today.

For example, the British Captain James Cook, whom you can read about in the *Australia and the South Pacific* volume of this series, was a highly regarded surveyor as well as a navigator. During the 1700s, he made extremely precise maps of the St. Lawrence River and the coast of Newfoundland. Cook became famous for his discoveries in the North and South Pacific Oceans, which helped mapmakers to complete the previously blank and inaccurate maps of those regions.

The First American Map

Of course, not all maps are made by people with first-hand knowledge of an area. As an example, look at the map on page 30. This is a portion of a 43 x 48-inch wall map produced in 1784 by a Connecticut silversmith and engraver named Abel Buell. His map was published just after the American Revolution ended, which made it the first map of America made by an American.

It is generally supposed that Buell copied most of his information from other maps of the time, which was a common practice. However, rather than include only the original states, Buell extended his map westward to the Mississippi River. His map helped stimulate plans to acquire, explore, and further map the western part of North America.

Lewis and Clark

Look at the 1805 map on page 34. At first you might think it is a much less important map than Buell's because it is just a simple sketch.

▼ *Below:* The famous explorers Meriwether Lewis and William Clark, at the mouth of the Columbia River, on the Pacific Coast.

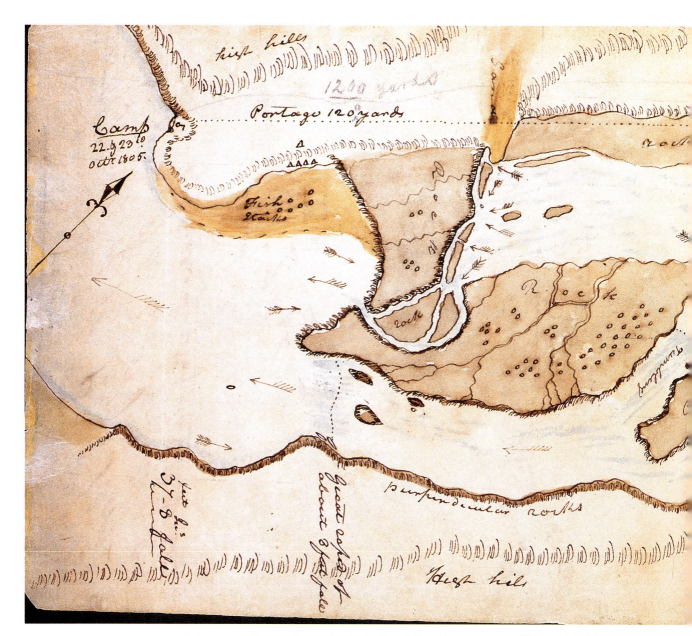

high hills

1200 yards

Portage 120 yards

Camp
22. & 23.
Octr 1805.

Fish
Stalls

R. o c k s

rock

perpendicular rocks

High hills

▲ **Above:** *This map, from the journals of Lewis and Clark, indicates where the Great Falls of the Columbia River are located.*

This map of a section of the Columbia River is actually a valuable historical document. It was made during the 28-month Lewis and Clark expedition—the first U.S. expedition into the lands west of the Mississippi River.

The journals of explorers Meriwether Lewis and William Clark contained hundreds of maps like this one as well as drawings and observations about this new area of the country. In 1814, Clark published a full map of the region. For the first time, the eastern and

western parts of the country were connected through mapped details.

Clark's map, connecting the known and unknown, prompted the beginning of western expansion in the United States. It stirred people's imaginations and offered them a route for following their dreams. Throughout the 1800s, this same exploration and mapping process was going on worldwide—both on land and at sea.

Promoting Exploration

The British sent out ships especially to make surveys of coastlines and coastal waters. On page 36 you will see a map based on a survey of the west coast of Africa made by Captain Edward Belcher between 1830 and 1832. The captain contributed data for scores of charts of not only the west coast of Africa, but also the Americas and the East Indies.

Many societies were formed during the 1800s to promote exploration in order to learn about and fill in the many blank areas that still existed on world maps. The African Association, for example, which was founded by an English botanist, was formally known as the Association for Promoting the Discovery of the Interior Parts of Africa.

In 1831 it merged with the one-year-old Geographical Society of London (later named the Royal Geographical Society). The Royal Geographical Society has helped fund many explorations over the

Left: This map of the west coast of Africa was based on the data collected by Captain Edward Belcher between 1830 and 1832.

years, and passes its information on to the public through lectures, publications, and, of course, maps.

In the United States, the National Geographic Society (NGS) has performed much the same functions. The NGS was organized in 1888 to "increase and diffuse geographic knowledge." Explorers received financial help for travels to the North Pole, the South Pole, and countless points in between. And, from the first, the Society's magazine included charts and maps to help readers see what the world was really like.

As time went on, mapping became increasingly important to the society and, in 1915, a separate cartographic division was formed to produce maps beyond those that went into *National Geographic* magazine.

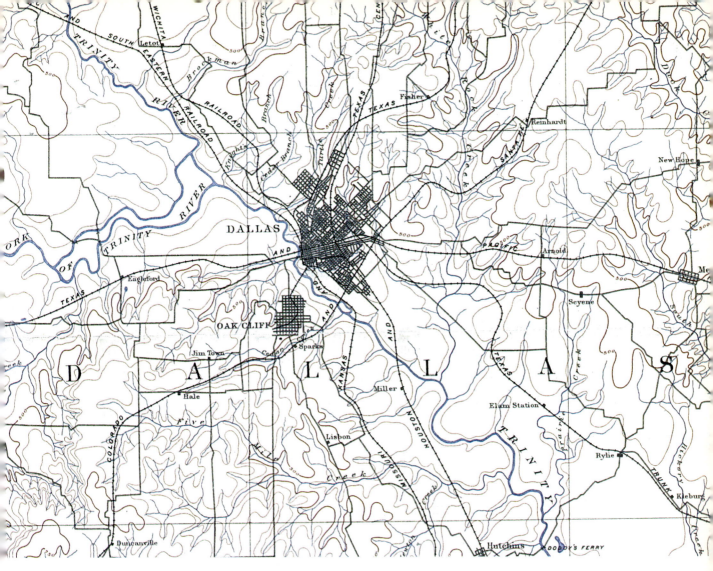

Commercial Maps

Throughout history, maps have helped governments, businesses, explorers, and scientists to do their work. Though the general public was probably interested in what the world looked like, maps were not widely available until the mid-1800s.

Ancient and medieval maps were drawn individually by hand—a slow process that limited the number of maps available and made them very expensive, when they were sold at all. Eventually, the process of printing from wooden blocks, which was invented in China in the 700s, made its way to Europe. By the late 1400s, European mapmakers were using wood-block printing to produce multiple copies of single maps, and maps became more accessible to the public.

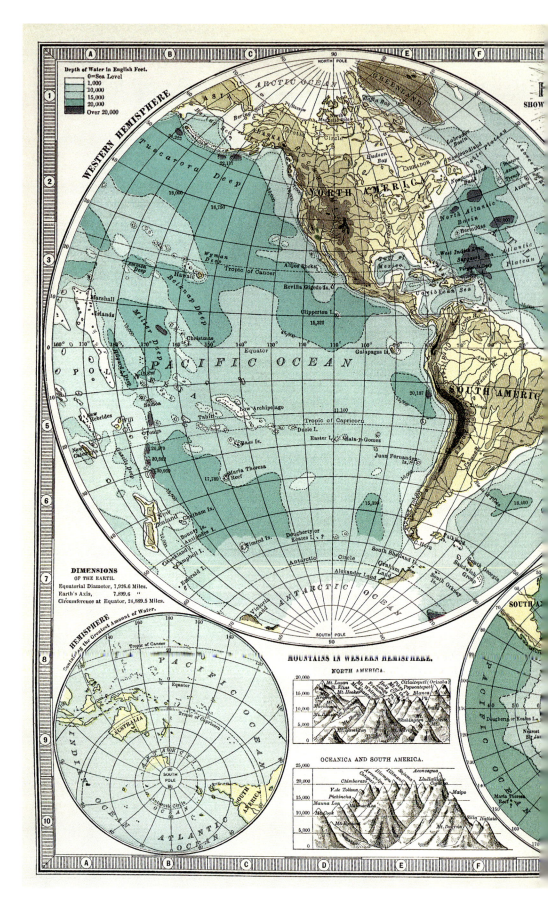

▶ **Right:** *This 1897 commercial map displays a great deal of information: land heights, ocean depths, and views of the North and South Poles.*

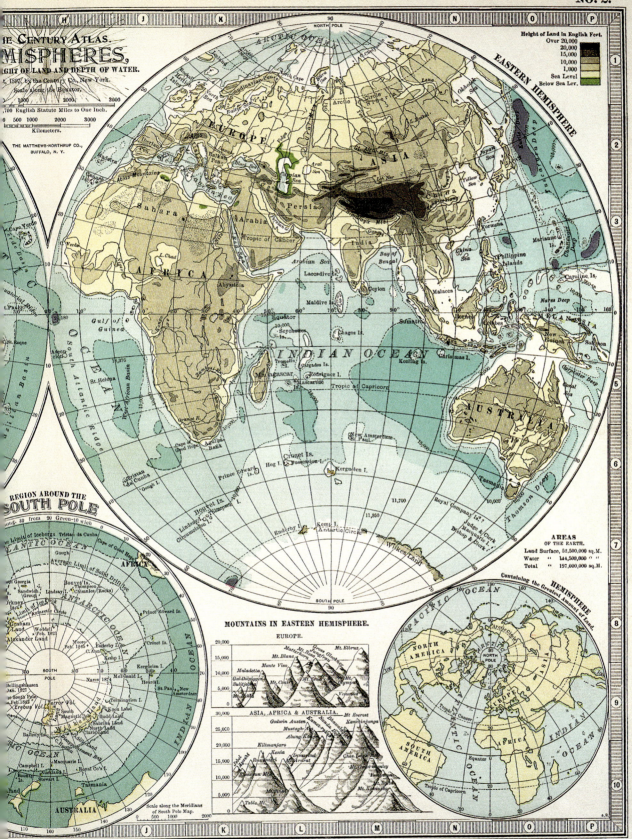

THE CENTURY ATLAS.

HEMISPHERES,
HEIGHT OF LAND AND DEPTH OF WATER.

1897, by the Century Co., New York.

Scale along the Equator.

1000   2000   3000

700 English Statute Miles to One Inch.

0 500 1000   2000   3000
Kilometers.

THE MATTHEWS-NORTHRUP CO.,
BUFFALO, N. Y.

Height of Land in English Feet.
Over 20,000
20,000
15,000
10,000
1,000
Sea Level
Below Sea Lev.

EASTERN HEMISPHERE

AREAS
OF THE EARTH.
Land Surface, 52,500,000 sq.M.
Water   "   144,500,000 "
Total   "   197,000,000 sq.M.

HEMISPHERE
Containing the Greatest Amount of Land

REGION AROUND THE
SOUTH POLE

MOUNTAINS IN EASTERN HEMISPHERE.

EUROPE.

ASIA, AFRICA & AUSTRALIA.

Scale along the Meridians
of South Pole Map.
500   1000   2000

In the mid-1500s, wood-block printing was replaced with copper-plate engraving. Cartographers could now make finer and more detailed maps. Engraving remained a popular method of printing for almost 300 years.

Then in the 1820s, lithography became the preferred printing method because it was faster and cheaper than engraving. In an engraving, the map was cut into the printing surface—for example, a sheet of copper. The printing surface was then covered with ink. When the ink was wiped off, the engraved lines remained filled with ink, and the map was transferred to a piece of paper. In lithography, the map was drawn on the printing surface with a grease or wax that would hold ink. The surface was inked, then rinsed. The drawn parts held the ink, and the image was transferred to a piece of paper. Flat, polished stones were the first lithographic printing surfaces.

Lithography was faster than engraving because it was easier to draw a map image *on* a surface than to cut it *into* the surface. And lithography was cheaper than engraving because stones (and later, metal plates) were less expensive than copper plates. Finally, there was a practical way to meet a growing demand for maps from people who were excited to see the world taking shape.

Maps continued to be hand painted, however, until a lithographic method of coloring was developed in 1860. The 1897 map of the hemispheres on pages 38–39 shows how the lithographic system of layered coloring was used to show land heights and ocean depths. This is an example of an early commercially produced map.

The 1893 topographic map of the Dallas, Texas, area shown on page 37 is from the same period. It was not a strictly commercial map, however. The map was produced by the U.S. Geological Survey (USGS). This organization began conducting topographic and geological surveys of the United States and producing its findings. Today, the USGS produces many types of maps, including topographic maps of the moon and of Mars, as well as satellite images such as the ones on pages 44, 47, and 48–49.

New Maps for New Forms of Transportation

It was not only the discovery and exploration of new lands that stimulated the desire for new maps. The invention of new modes of transportation created another market for the art of the mapmaker. The growth of Rand McNally as a mapmaker, for example, stemmed from the growth of railroading and, later, automobiles in the United States.

Rand McNally

The early business of Rand McNally & Company consisted of printing railroad passenger tickets, timetables, and guides. The first Rand McNally map showed the route of a single railroad and was included in the December 1872 "Railway Guide," a guide to railroad lines. As train travel continued to grow, travelers demanded more maps showing where, exactly, they were going. Rand McNally turned its efforts to meeting that demand.

In the early 1900s, the company's attention focused on a new mode of transportation: the automobile. Before it published road maps, Rand McNally produced photo auto guides. These were collections of photographs taken along a route. The first guide was for a route between Chicago and Milwaukee. To create the guide, Andrew McNally II and his wife drove along, taking pictures the whole way! In 1917, Rand McNally published the first road map for motorists that identified highways by numbers. It was a map of Illinois, and it was soon followed by similar maps of the nation's road system.

Rand McNally's approach was revolutionary. The company sent people into the field not only to map the highways, but also to post them with numbers that matched those marked on a map. The modern road map—and highway system—were born.

Airplanes Lend a New Perspective

New forms of transportation had a strong impact on mapmaking, and airplanes were no exception. When combined with photography, the effect was revolutionary.

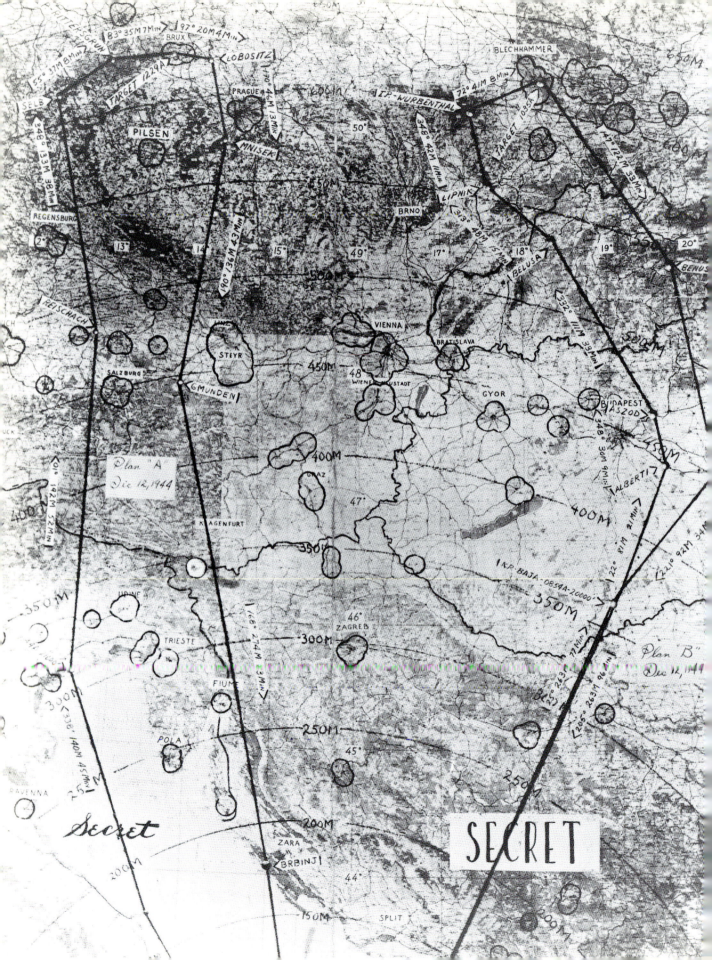

Photography was invented in 1839, and some aerial photographs were made from hot-air balloons as early as the 1850s. But it wasn't until airplanes came into wide use during World War I (1914–1918) that aerial photography became practical.

During the war, most aerial photos taken for military purposes were used as is; they were not used to make maps. The development of photogrammetric cameras in the 1920s and 1930s, however, made aerial mapping a reality. These special cameras were designed so that locations could be precisely pinpointed on pictures that were taken. As a mapping breakthrough, it could be compared to the invention of the chronometer in the 1700s, which allowed precise ocean mapping for the first time.

During World War II (1939–45), maps constructed from aerial photographs were used to plan many military campaigns. On the opposite page you can see a bombing map of eastern Europe.

After World War II, aerial photography was widely used for surveying. In combination with radar (bouncing radio signals off a target and recording the return signals) this bird's-eye view allowed the first detailed, accurate maps to be made of many parts of South America, Africa, and even the United States. Because radar could "see" beneath tropical forest cover, heavy clouds, and even at night, it added an immense amount of information to the world's maps.

A Closer Look

By looking at the information contained on a map, you can gain a sense of what was important to the mapmaker—why the map was made. Look again at the 1893 map of Dallas on page 37. What features are emphasized on this map? Who would be interested in such details? Compare this map with a current map of the same area. What differences stand out? What might this tell you about why each map was made?

◀◀ *Opposite: During World War II, bomber pilots used maps such as this one of Central and Eastern Europe in order to locate their targets.*

Chapter 3

The Future of Mapmaking

The future of mapmaking was first glimpsed in the mid-1900s, when relatively new technologies, such as sonar and computers, held great promise for mapmakers. In addition, the first satellites gave cartographers a better view of not only our world but also of other worlds. Mapmakers discovered that they could construct their maps in a way not even imagined 50 years earlier.

Sonar

Sonar involves the use of sound waves to detect objects. The length of time it takes the waves to be sent out, reach the object, and bounce back to a receiver is recorded. This can be translated into a distance measurement. Although sonar was invented in the early 1900s, it wasn't until the middle of the century that it was used to study and map the ocean floor. You can read about this in the *Oceans and Skies* volume of this series.

Sonar greatly increased the accuracy of early nautical charts. A modern chart is shown on page 46. Notice how closely spaced the soundings (depth measurements) are.

◀◀ *Opposite: This satellite image of Baghdad was taken in 1991 during the Persian Gulf War.*

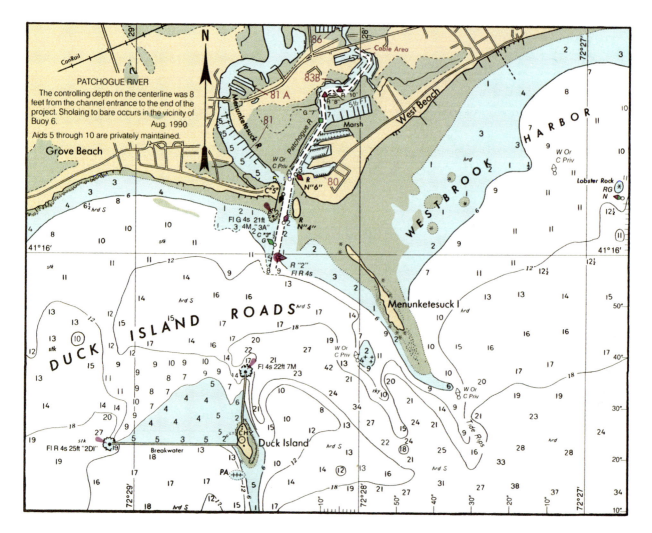

▲ *Above:* This nautical chart of a portion of the Long Island Sound along the Connecticut shoreline is based on information that was obtained with sonar equipment.

Satellites

The first satellite was launched into Earth's orbit by the Soviet Union (now the Commonwealth of Independent States) in 1957. In the nearly half century since then, space programs have been directed toward discovering and recording as much information as possible about our world and the universe around us.

Satellites carry cameras to take pictures of Earth. They also carry remote-sensing equipment—such as thermometers, sonar, and radar—that transmit specialized information back to Earth. The information is transcribed into maps, charts, or other data formats.

Satellite-based scanners read electromagnetic waves emitted from Earth's surface to provide data that can be translated by a computer into a variety of visual images. The images can distinguish buildings from natural features, or show different crops in an agricultural landscape. They can even show where polluted water ends up after it leaves a factory. Look at the illustration below. Although this looks like an aerial photograph of Antarctica, it is actually an example of satellite imaging—a computer-generated satellite "picture." The satellite's scanners transmit information that can then be colored to show the difference between, for example, snow, ice, and bare rock. By overlaying this image with geographic labels, it can be transformed into a map.

▼ *Below:* This satellite image of Antarctica is called a "mosaic." It was created with the aid of a computer from 23 satellite images.

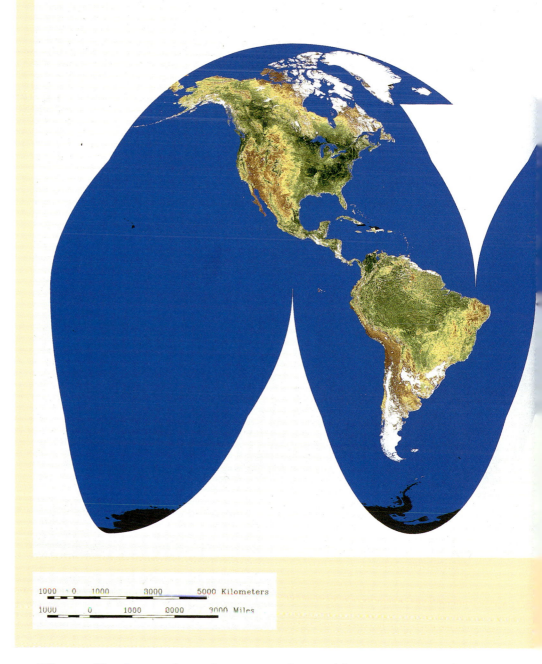

▶ Right: *This map shows the distribution of Earth's vegetation. It was produced from almost 100 daily observations that were transmitted via satellite during a nine-day period.*

1000   0   1000   3000   5000 Kilometers

1000   0   1000   2000   3000 Miles

The satellite image above focuses on the world's vegetation. The satellite image of Baghdad, Iraq, shown on page 44 was taken during the Persian Gulf War. The Tigris River flows diagonally across the picture; the city straddles the river just to the right of center.

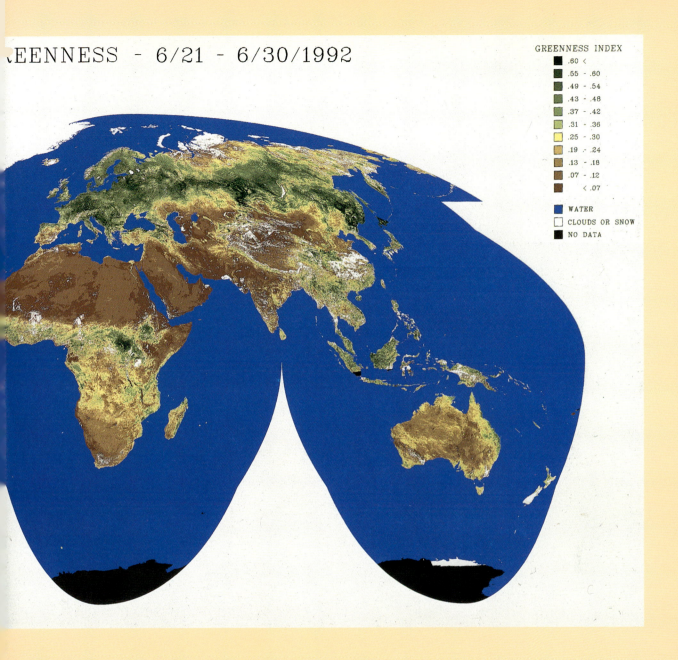

GREENNESS INDEX

■	.60 <
■	.55 - .60
■	.49 - .54
■	.43 - .48
■	.37 - .42
■	.31 - .36
■	.25 - .30
■	.19 - .24
■	.13 - .18
■	.07 - .12
■	< .07
■	WATER
□	CLOUDS OR SNOW
■	NO DATA

As you can begin to see from these examples, everything from topographic maps to resource maps, place maps to weather maps, are constructed from satellite data. This technology has helped people get a better understanding of the world they live in.

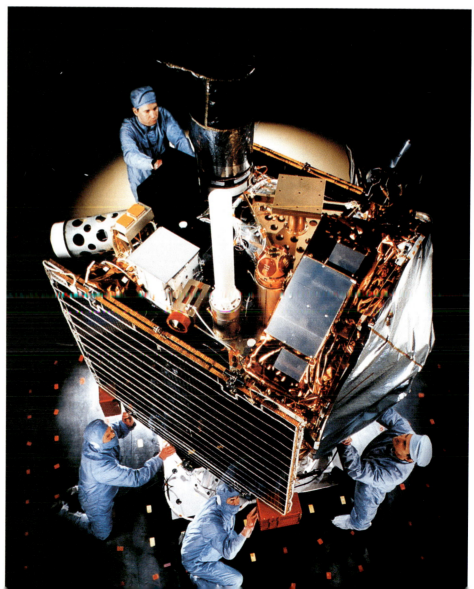

▲ *Top:* *In this photograph of Mars taken from the Pathfinder,* the rover Sojourner *is "studying" a large rock on the right.*

▶ *Right:* The Mars Global Surveyor *is doing a mapping survey of the planet. The large cylinder at the top, in the center, is the Mars Orbiter Camera, which transmits images from Mars daily.*

50

Mapping Our Solar System

People have been studying and mapping the skies since ancient times. The dawn of the space age in the mid-1900s, however, allowed scientists to begin examining and mapping our solar system and the universe in detail. The first target for study was the moon.

Between 1966 and 1977, the United States sent satellites into orbit around the moon. These lunar orbiters sent back images of the moon, including its far side, which we never see from Earth. The images were then used to obtain accurate measurements of the moon's surface for the creation of topographically accurate maps. Additional information was obtained from the manned *Apollo* missions to the moon. Photographs and scientific data provided the basis for a wide variety of maps of even greater detail.

Mars: A New Frontier

With the successful exploration of the moon, it was only a small step to exploring the planets, and beyond. Space probes (unmanned spacecraft sent to probe the universe) relay large quantities of information back to Earth, from which maps can be constructed. Planetary landers provide even more information through direct contact with and exploration of a planet. Most recently, Mars has become the focus of a great deal of attention. It is the most likely place for humans to establish colonies in space. Two recent NASA (National Aeronautics and Space Administration) efforts at exploring Mars are shown in the illustrations on pages 50 and 53.

The image on the top of page 50 was taken by the 1997 planetary lander *Pathfinder*, whose rear ramp can be seen in the lower left. A robotic rover named *Sojourner* traveled down that ramp and onto the Martian surface to examine the dust and rocks. You can see *Sojourner's* tracks leading away from the ramp, and the rover itself taking readings of the large rock on the right.

The illustration on page 53 is an artist's view of the *Mars Global Surveyor* spacecraft, which was sent to Mars in the fall of 1997. The craft will orbit the planet for two Earth years (one Martian year) doing a mapping survey: taking pictures, monitoring the weather, and determining the kinds and distribution of minerals.

As newer and more advanced probes turn their lenses and sensors deeper into space, the data they send back will enable scientists to draw a clearer picture, and a better map, of the universe as we know it and as it was at the beginning of time.

◄ *Left: An artist's picture of the* Mars Global Surveyor *in orbit.*

Computers

Photography, airplanes, sonar, and space technology have changed both how and what we map, but computers have had the biggest impact on cartography.

The first computer-generated map to be published was a simple weather map that was constructed in 1950. Since that time, computers have become a standard part of most mapmaking efforts, and the results are often anything but simple! Computer-generated maps can include a wide array of special effects, such as the three-dimensional map on the right, showing U.S. earthquake zones.

This map was designed by Dr. Melvin Pruitt, a physicist at the Los Alamos National Laboratory, in New Mexico. Pruitt wrote the computer program that he used to create the map. He wanted to show the probability of an earthquake occurring in various parts of the country. The places with the

▶ *Right: On this computer-generated map, the highest peaks indicate regions that are most likely to have earthquakes. The tall peak below the Great Lakes is in Missouri, along the Mississippi River.*

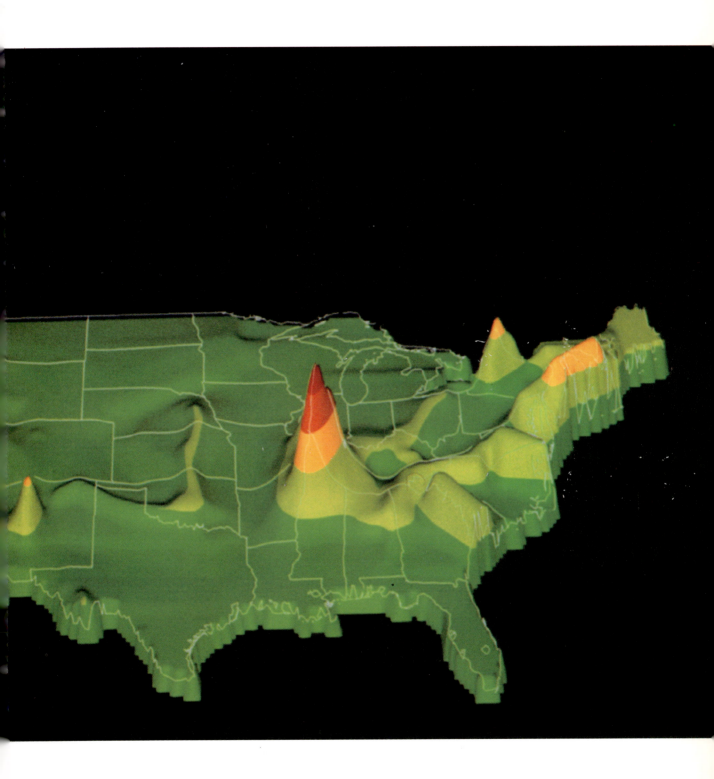

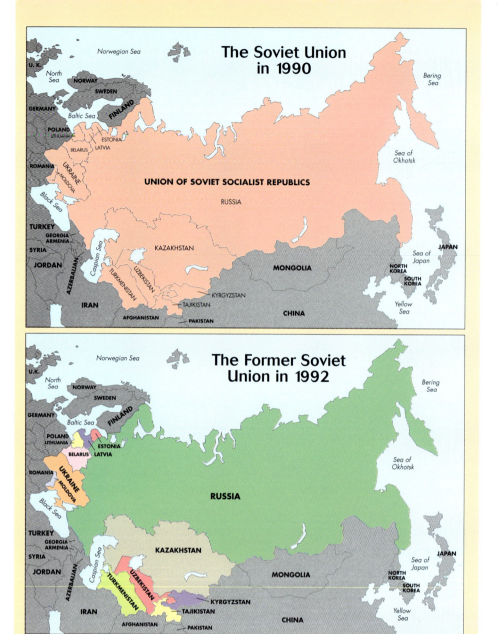

The Soviet Union in 1990

UNION OF SOVIET SOCIALIST REPUBLICS

The Former Soviet Union in 1992

▶ *Right: Computerized maps allow a mapmaker to easily change boundaries or country names or both when a political change occurs. The top map shows the former Soviet Union before 1991. The bottom map shows this same region after the twelve republics became independent nations.*

highest peaks are most likely to have an earthquake. The map allows scientists to compare various regions at a glance, without having to look through pages of statistics.

Computers are used to record, store, and arrange data. As we have seen, they can even do this work on board orbiting satellites or other spacecraft. Cartographers can pull up and arrange the data they need on a computer terminal, either from a series of databanks or by using sophisticated geographic information systems (GIS) software. Some mapping companies even design their own systems. For instance, Hammond Incorporated created an extensive digital database and, in 1992, published the first computer-generated world atlas.

Digital map sets are now available which can be modified to create unique, detailed maps relatively easily. The maps are orginally created by cartographers, but they can be modified into a variety of different formats by someone who doesn't have mapmaking training (such as a graphic designer). The physical maps of the continents used in this series were created from digital map sets. The examples in the Appendix on page 56 show the four stages in the creation of the physical map of Africa used in the *Africa* volume.

Using computers allows cartographers to turn out accurate maps more easily and quickly than ever before by rearranging stored data. This allows them to keep pace with world changes, such as the breakup of the Soviet Union, illustrated by the maps on the opposite page.

As you have seen, cartography is an ever-changing science. It reflects the frontiers of our knowledge about the world and the universe, recording information in a form that is easy for people to understand. As long as we remain curious about our world and our place in it, we will need maps to show us that world and to guide us through it.

A Closer Look

Mapping techniques and technology advanced by great leaps in the second half of the 1900s. Compare the B-17 bomber map from World War II (page 42) and the satellite image of Baghdad, Iraq, during the Persian Gulf War (page 44). The second map was made nearly 50 years later than the first. What does the level of detail tell you about the technology used to create both maps? Mention specific points that you feel makes one map more useful than the other.

Appendix: Creating a Physical Map from a Digital Map Set

STEP 1: *This base map was adapted from aerial photographs. It shows shadows caused by elevation. The mapmaker can decide how dark the shadows should be.*

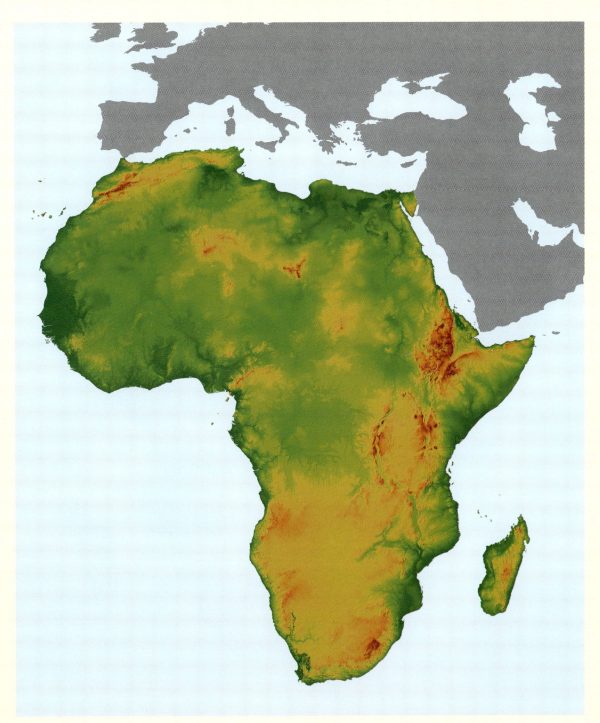

STEP 2: *A color overlay is added to the base map. The colors are coded to give the reader more precise information about elevation than the base map can give. On this map, the darkest brown indicates the highest elevation, but the mapmaker can change the color scheme.*

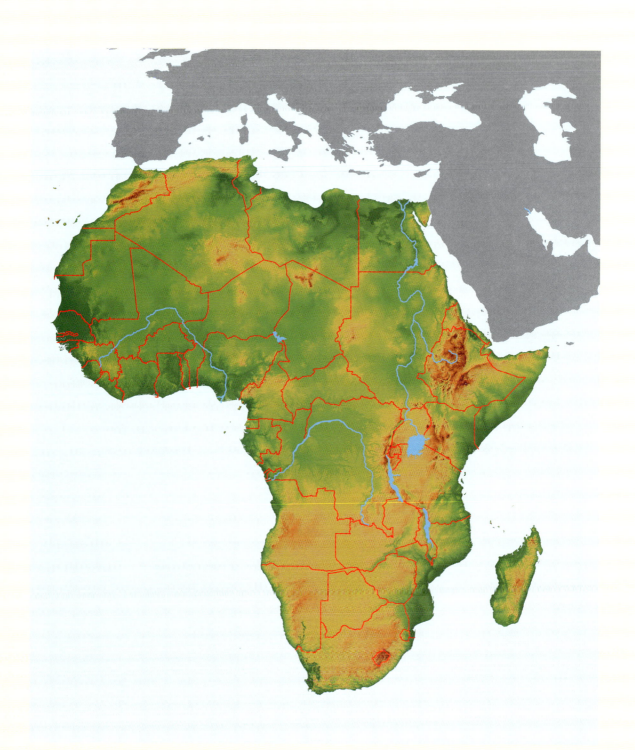

STEP 3: *With the color overlay in place, the mapmaker adds political boundaries and bodies of water. The color and thickness of the boundaries are up to the mapmaker.*

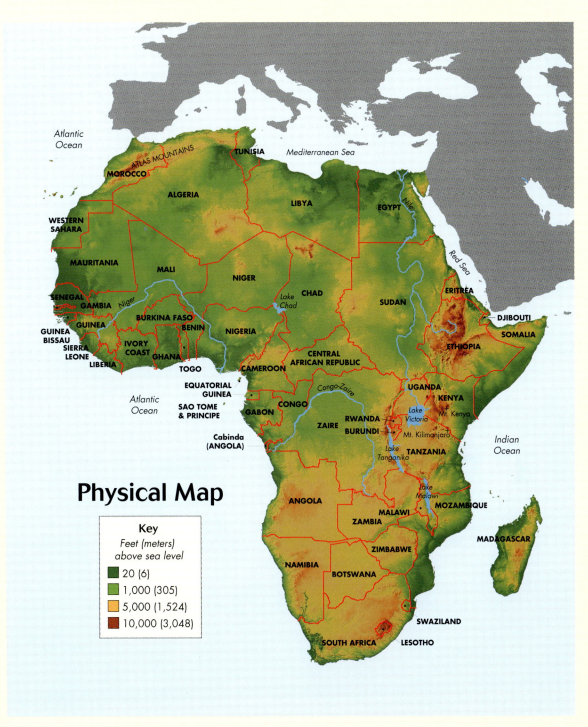

Physical Map

Key

Feet (meters) above sea level

- 20 (6)
- 1,000 (305)
- 5,000 (1,524)
- 10,000 (3,048)

Atlantic Ocean

ATLAS MOUNTAINS

TUNISIA

Mediterranean Sea

MOROCCO

ALGERIA

LIBYA

EGYPT

Nile

WESTERN SAHARA

Red Sea

MAURITANIA

MALI

NIGER

CHAD

Lake Chad

SUDAN

ERITREA

DJIBOUTI

SENEGAL

Niger

GAMBIA

BURKINA FASO

BENIN

NIGERIA

SOMALIA

GUINEA

ETHIOPIA

GUINEA BISSAU

SIERRA LEONE

IVORY COAST

GHANA

TOGO

CENTRAL AFRICAN REPUBLIC

LIBERIA

CAMEROON

UGANDA

KENYA

EQUATORIAL GUINEA

Congo-Zaire

Mt. Kenya

Atlantic Ocean

SAO TOME & PRINCIPE

CONGO

GABON

ZAIRE

RWANDA

BURUNDI

Lake Victoria

Mt. Kilimanjaro

Indian Ocean

Cabinda (ANGOLA)

Lake Tanganika

TANZANIA

Lake Malawi

ANGOLA

MALAWI

MOZAMBIQUE

ZAMBIA

MADAGASCAR

ZIMBABWE

NAMIBIA

BOTSWANA

SWAZILAND

SOUTH AFRICA

LESOTHO

STEP 4: *This map of Africa would not be complete without labels. The mapmaker chooses the position, size and color of the type, as well as the style of the type, which is called the typeface. The labels on this map were created in typefaces called Futura and Cosmos.*

Glossary

aerial photographs Photographs taken from an aircraft.

astrolabe An instrument used by navigators to establish latitude by measuring the altitude of the sun.

atlas A collection of maps bound into a single book.

cartographer A person who makes maps.

chronometer A clock that can accurately measure time at sea. It is used to establish longitude.

compass An instrument with a needle that always points north. It is used to help tell direction.

cross-staff An instrument used to establish latitude by measuring the altitude of the sun.

grid A framework of squares used to help locate points on a map.

latitude Imaginary lines that run around Earth parallel to the equator. They are used to locate points north and south of the equator.

longitude Imaginary lines that run at right angles to the equator and meet at the North and South Poles. They are used to locate points east and west of the prime meridian.

nautical Having to do with the navigation of ships.

photogrammetric camera A camera designed so that locations can be precisely pinpointed from aerial photographs taken with the camera.

portolan chart A map for navigators produced during the Middle Ages.

prime meridian The line of 0 degrees longitude that passes through Greenwich, England.

projection A way of representing a round Earth on a flat surface.

quadrant A refinement of the cross-staff that could be used with one's back to the sun.

scale The relationship of distance on a map to the actual distance on the ground.

sextant An instrument similar to a quadrant but smaller and easier to use in order to establish latitude.

sonar The use of sound waves to detect objects.

surveying Determining the size, shape, and position of an area by measuring the angles and distances between sets of points.

topographic map A map that shows the elevation of features in relation to each other.

wind rose A circular design that shows the directions from which the winds blow.

Further Reading

Buisseret, David, ed. *From Sea Charts to Satellite Images: Interpreting North American History Through Maps.* Chicago: University of Chicago Press, 1990.

Carlisle, Madelyn Wood. *Let's Investigatge Marvelously Meaningful Maps.* Hauppauge, NY: Barron, 1992.

Ganeri, Anita. *The Story of Maps and Navigation.* New York: Oxford University Press, 1997.

Glicksman, Jane. *Cool Geography.* New York: Putnam Publishing Group, 1998.

Mango, Karin N. *Mapmaking.* New York: Jullian Messner, 1984.

Ryan, Peter. *Explorers and Mapmakers.* New York: E.P. Dutton, 1990.

Smith, A.G. *Where Am I? The Story of Maps and Navigation.* _____: Stoddart Kids Publishing, 1997.

Stefoff, Rebecca. *The Young Oxford Companion to Maps and Mapmaking.* New York: Oxford University Press, 1995.

Weiss, Harvey. Maps: *Getting From Here to There.* Boston: Houghton Mifflin Company, 1991.

Whitfield, Peter. *New Found Lands: Maps in the History of Exploration.* New York: Routledge, 1998.

Index

Page numbers for illustrations are in boldface.